ENGINEERS DID IT!

ENGINEERS DID IT!

by DUANE BRADLEY

Illustrated by ANNE MARIE JAUSS

J. B. LIPPINCOTT COMPANY
Philadelphia and New York

BY THE SAME AUTHOR:

CAPPY AND THE JET ENGINE

CONTENTS

ENGINEERS DID IT!

1

MEN WITH WINGS ON THEIR MINDS

What is an engineer?

If you were an engineer, how would your work be different from other people's?

Engineers build bridges, make roads, design airplanes, dig tunnels, and make the exciting rides you like at amusement parks. They work on the very tiny parts of a television set, and on the huge dams that hold mighty rivers. Their jobs may be in the town where you live, or anywhere in the world.

There is a word in our language called ingenuity. It means being able to find a way to do things. Engineering and ingenuity are alike, because the important thing about an engineer is that he finds a way to do things that seem impossible.

Suppose that a very rich man bought a home in a desert, and wanted a swimming pool. An engineer would find a way to bring water for the pool into the dry land. Some engineers have found a way to launch a world satellite.

Engineering is solving problems. Ever since the world began, engineers have been finding ways to use what we have to make life better. They made bows and arrows that would kill more game than rocks thrown by hand. They invented concrete to make buildings and bridges that have lasted for thousands of years. When you make something that works, or find a better way to do something, you are engineering.

This book is about some of the things engineers have done, and when you read it you will learn something else about engineers. They are men with wings on their minds. These wings are courage and imagination—when an engineer decides that a job is not too big for him, and starts finding a way to do it, he is using his wings.

An engineer works with many tools, and with every kind of material there is in our world. No matter where he is, or what he is doing, his main job is to make our world a better one for us.

2

THE OLDEST SKYSCRAPER
IN THE WORLD

Skyscrapers are buildings so tall that they seem to touch the sky. The first one we know about was built more than five thousand years ago, before men had electricity, power tools, or any sort of motors to help them.

It was about the year 3000 B.C. in the warm sunny country of Egypt. The ruler of Egypt was the Pharaoh Cheops.

Cheops, like the Pharaohs who had lived before him, had great wealth and unlimited power. Everything that he saw belonged to him, and his every wish was granted. He was not only the ruler of his country, but his people worshipped him as a god.

The Egyptians believed in a life after death.

9

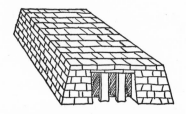 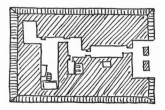

THE OUTSIDE OF AN EGYPTIAN TOMB OR MASTABAH AND
A PLAN OF ITS INTERIOR

They thought that when they died they would go
into another world very much like this one and
would live again as they had lived here. Everything
that was buried with them in their tombs would go
with them into the new life.

Wealthy Egyptians had very large and beautiful
tombs built for themselves, and spent most of their
lives seeing that they were as fine as possible. Like
other Pharaohs, Cheops had work begun on his
own tomb as soon as he came to the throne.

For many years before this, the tombs of wealthy
Egyptians were called mastabahs. They were made
of stone, and looked like very large boxes with sides
which slanted outward. Inside they were almost
solid, except for one or two small rooms and a
tunnel which led to the burial chamber.

One Pharaoh, named Zoser, had his mastabah begun, and then had an idea. He wanted it to be larger and more splendid than any other that existed, so that he would be even more powerful in the next world. The first layer of huge stone blocks was made larger so that it covered more ground. The next layer was a little smaller so that from the outside it looked like a step. Layer after layer of stone was added, each one square but smaller than the one below. The finished building rose two hundred feet into the air—a square built to a pointed top. . This was a mastabah different from any other. The Egyptians called it a pyramid.

ZOSER BUILT HIS TOMB IN THE SHAPE OF A PYRAMID

When Cheops came to the throne he wanted a pyramid for himself, but one even bigger than Zoser's. He wanted his tomb to be the largest ever built, and one that would last forever.

He chose the spot on which it would stand, a hill named Giza. The material would, of course, be stone, since stone was plentiful and longer-lasting than anything else. The design was simple—huge blocks of stone were to be cut and fitted together, much as they were in Zoser's tomb. Cheops, who had great wealth and power, probably saw no reason why he should not have exactly the sort of pyramid he wanted.

Engineers who study the remains of this giant pyramid today know that it was not so simple. Even now, with all of the powerful machines and equipment we have, building a pyramid would be very difficult.

We do not know exactly how the pyramid of Cheops was built, but we do know that more than wealth and power was needed for the job. The engineering skill of people who lived so long ago made it possible.

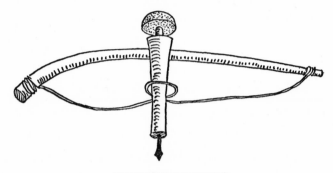

AN EGYPTIAN DRILL

The Egyptians were clever people and good work-men. They were not inventors, but they knew how to use ideas from other years and other countries. They had certain tools like those we have today, such as hammers, chisels, saws and drills. These tools were quite simple and not nearly as good as ours. The Egyptian drill looked like a bow and arrow, with the "arrow" as the drill. A jewel was set in the point of the drill so that it would be harder than the stone on which it was used, and would cut better. The string of the bow was wound once or twice around the drill so that when the bow was moved back and forth the string wound and unwound, turning the drill, which bored into the stone.

Probably the large stones to be cut from the quarry were measured and marked. Drills were used to make a row of holes on the outside of the stone. This weakened the stone on that line, so that it could be split out by use of wedges or chisels.

The rough stone was then loaded onto a stone rocker. This was a strong wooden platform with heavy wooden rockers, like those on a rocking chair. The rockers could be tilted back and forth so that the stone could be worked on more easily, and either end could be raised by using a lever under it.

A STONE ROCKER

AN ANCIENT EGYPTIAN DRAWING OF MASONS AT WORK

The Egyptians had different tools for measuring the surface of the rock so that it could be made smooth and even. One of these was a set of four short rods, all the same length. A cord was tied to the tops of two of them which were stood upright as far apart as they would go. The others were moved under the cord along the top of the stone to find where it was uneven. Another tool looked like a huge letter A with a weighted cord hung from the peak of the A. When the two legs of this tool were set on a block of stone, the cord hung down. If it hung exactly in the center, the stone was even; if it hung to one side or the other the stone was uneven and needed more leveling.

Each stone was cut to go in a certain place in the pyramid. The surrounding stones were cut to fit it perfectly. This was done at the quarry, and each stone was marked so that it could be put in place when it was taken to the pyramid.

After the stone was cut exactly to the right size with its sides perfectly smooth, it had to be moved to the site of the pyramid. As a pyramid was built higher and higher the stone had to be lifted into place. Today, it would be loaded on huge trucks or trains and hauled to where it was needed. Power cranes would be used to lift it. The Egyptians had no such equipment, but only their brains and muscles.

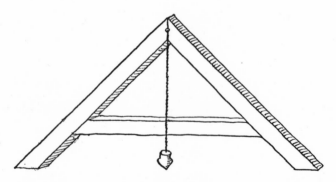

THE EGYPTIANS USED THIS TOOL TO FIND OUT IF
A STONE WAS LEVEL

They had what are called simple machines which work as well today as they did then. A simple machine is not a motor, but something which increases what a man can do. No matter how strong a man is, his muscles alone can do only so much work. A simple machine increases this amount of work.

The inclined plane is one kind of simple machine. An inclined plane is a slanted surface. A stone that cannot be pushed along the ground can be rolled down hill. It is easier to push a heavy weight up a slanted surface than to lift it straight into the air. Steps and stairs are another use of the inclined plane. Few of us could climb straight up a wall, but all of us can walk up stairs. Chisels and axes and saws are all inclined planes—their thin cutting edge, which is a slanted surface, cuts better than a dull edge.

A lever is another simple machine. If one end of a board is put under the edge of a large stone and a smaller stone shoved beneath the board, it becomes a lever. By pushing down on the opposite end of the board, a great deal of force can be used to raise the stone.

The Egyptians must have used levers to help raise the huge stone blocks onto sledges, which were like flat-bottomed sleds. It is possible that they used logs under the sledges as rollers, or long wheels, to make them easier to move. Perhaps they poured water on the path the sledges were to follow, since a wet slippery surface would make the hauling easier.

A great deal of the granite used for the pyramid was cut out of the stone quarry at Giza, but some of it had to be brought from another quarry farther up the Nile River. This stone was floated down the river on barges.

One of the most amazing things about the Great Pyramid was the huge inclined plane, or mammoth ramp, which was built. This was a road which slanted from the edge of the Nile up to the base of the pyramid. Stone was loaded on sledges at the base of the ramp, then slowly hauled up to the place it was needed. Perhaps the end of the ramp next to the pyramid was built higher and higher as work progressed so that stone could be brought to the right working level.

Some historians believe that the Egyptians used another simple machine, called an A-frame, to raise blocks of stones from one layer to another. This was a kind of pulley with the frames shaped like the letter A, with ropes hanging from it. When the legs of the A were fastened firmly to the stone, men could pull huge weights by hauling on the ropes.

It is said that it took 100,000 men twenty years to build the pyramid of Cheops, and that it took at least ten years to build the huge ramp. The stones weighed many tons, and were cut so perfectly that a knife blade could not have been slipped between them when they were in place. When the pyramid was finished, one side was not more than a fraction of an inch longer than another.

The pyramid of Cheops was larger and more beautiful than Zoser's tomb and its sides were perfectly flat and even. Cheops had his workmen cut granite blocks to fit into the "steps" on the side to make the surfaces flat.

For more than five thousand years the Great Pyramid has stood on the hill of Giza, worn now by time and weather. It is still a wonder and a puzzle to mankind. Through all of these centuries men have traveled from all over the world to stand and gaze at it, and to ask themselves how the Egyptians could have built it.

We still do not know the answer, but we realize what an astounding building it is. We do know that the Pharaoh Cheops wished for the largest tomb the world had even seen, and wanted it to last forever. The engineers of ancient Egypt made his dream come true.

THE PYRAMID OF CHEOPS

3

THE MAN WHO MADE A MOUNTAIN

Babylonia was a land without stones. Even a small pebble was quite rare, and considered a lucky thing to have.

It was a hot flat country where all green things except large trees grew well because they were watered by the Euphrates River. The people of Babylonia, like the people of Egypt, wanted to make huge buildings. Since they had neither stone nor good lumber, they had to use something else. They could not make trees, but they learned to make a kind of stone.

Perhaps, long long ago, a child dug clay from the ground and made toys with it. When he tired of the game, he left what he had made and went to something else. When he came back later, he saw that the clay dried by the sun was quite hard.

Perhaps another time a woman dropped a clay bowl into the fire over which she was cooking, and it broke. When the fire had cooled, she saw that the clay which had been heated by the fire was even harder than that dried by the sun. In some way like this, man learned to make bricks—and bricks are man-made stones.

The Babylonians had many fine clays which made excellent bricks. Some of them they dried in the sun, and others they baked, or fired, in ovens.

Bricks are not so large or so heavy as the stones used by Egyptians to build the pyramid. If they were merely piled up one on top of the other, they would fall down easily. They had to be held together in some way.

Our brick buildings are made with mortar, which is a kind of cement. The Babylonians did not have cement, but used something called bitumen. This was tar that had seeped to the surface of the ground from oil deposits beneath and had hardened. It was melted by heating and put between the bricks while it was still hot. As it cooled it became hard and held the bricks securely.

With their man-made stones and their natural mortar, the Babylonians made many huge and beautiful buildings. They used different kinds of clays to make bricks of different colors; and they found ways to coat the bricks and make them more durable and attractive. These coatings were called glazes and made a hard, shiny surface on the outside of the bricks.

Babylonia was a large, powerful country which lasted for many centuries. It was so wealthy that wars were fought over it. Once it was ruled by a nation called the Assyrians.

SOME BRICKS WERE DRIED IN THE SUN

The Babylonians tried to revolt so they could rule their own country. The Assyrians became so angry that they destroyed the city of Babylon completely. Their ruler said that he "pulled down, dug up, and burned with fire the town and palaces, root and branch; destroyed the fortress and the double wall, the temples of the gods and the towers of brick, and threw the rubbish into the river." The city was gone—but the Babylonians did not give up.

In about the year 626 B.C., more than twenty-five hundred years ago, they revolted again. Their leader was a man called Nabopolassar; and this time they won.

Nabopolassar was not born in Babylonia, but was an outsider. The people of Babylonia knew he was a brave soldier, and he wanted them to think of him as a great ruler. To make them happy under his rule, he planned to make the city of Babylon the most wonderful the world had ever seen.

He had large and beautiful buildings made of the native bricks. His own son, Nebuchadnezzar, was put to work as a bricklayer's helper, so he could learn how the jobs were done.

In time, Nabopolassar died and his son Nebuchadnezzar became ruler. He wanted to continue the work his father had begun.

If you have seen large cities, you know that many of them seem to have grown by accident. Perhaps people first moved to the spot because of a river which gave water for gardens and a way of travel. More people moved in, and more houses were built. Stores were put up, churches and schools were added, and as land became worth more, the city became more crowded. Most large cities have narrow streets, stores close to homes, and little room for parks and trees.

Nebuchadnezzar wanted a city that would be fitted to the people in it, and make their lives more pleasant. Today he would be called a planning engineer.

Since there were many wars in his time, a city had to be protected against its enemies. A huge wall was built around Babylon—wide enough at the top so that chariots could drive on it. The gates in the wall were made so strong that, when they were closed, enemies could not break through.

One way of waging war in those days was to

surround a city and lay siege to it. Cities which could not get food from outside were in danger of being starved to defeat, no matter how well they could fight. Nebuchadnezzar thought about this when he planned his city.

He made Babylon square, with each side of the outer wall fifteen miles long. Through the middle of the square ran the Euphrates River, which supplied the city with water. Ditches and canals were dug from the river to carry water where it was needed.

The streets, which were wide and straight, divided the city into smaller squares. Houses were built around the outside of the squares, and the land inside them was kept for gardens and parks. Some of the buildings were apartment houses where several families could live, but enough land was kept to raise food for the city. An enemy could stay outside the walls for a very long time without bothering the people of the planned city.

Babylon was one of the wonders of the ancient world. It was a large and busy place, and it was also beautiful. Nebuchadnezzar was not only one of the very first planning engineers, but he was also a good one.

Besides building a model city, he did something else to astonish the world.

His wife was a Median, from a mountainous country. She loved Babylon, but often she was homesick for her native mountains. Babylon was flat—there were no hills, no tall trees, nothing but an endless plain which stretched as far as her eyes could see.

Nebuchadnezzar wanted to please his wife, so he decided to build a mountain for her.

It was not to be just a tall pile of stone, or a solid building like the pyramids. It was to be beautiful, and covered with growing things.

He had it made of arches—wide doorways curved at the top and joined together. Each story of arches was topped by another until the man-made mountain rose three hundred fifty feet into the air. Now the homesick queen had something to look at to remind her of home—but Nebuchadnezzar had not finished.

As the men were building, he had them make the

roof of each story of arches with great care. First they were covered with reeds, then with hot bitumen, then with thick sheets of lead. When this was done, the roofs were watertight.

THE MOUNTAIN WAS CALLED THE HANGING GARDENS OF BABYLON

In the center of the building was a shaft, like an elevator shaft in a modern building. Under it were three very deep shafts going down into the earth: a square one in the middle and an oblong one on each side. Water was brought up these shafts from the river Euphrates to the gardens that were planted on the roofs.

We are not sure just how this was done. Perhaps there was an endless chain of buckets turned by a treadmill. After each bucket was filled with water, it was lifted up the chain to the top where its load was emptied into a huge cistern.

A kind of icebox, or refrigerator, was made in the building. It was known that water stayed cool longer than air, so special rooms were built near the water system where food could be kept.

Earth was put on each roof of the building, and flowers, grass, shrubs and even trees were grown there. A large moat was dug around the outside of the building and kept full of water. The hot breezes of the city, blown across the water in the moat, were cooled before they reached the tower.

Imagine the queen of Babylon when she entered her new treasure for the first time. She went from the hot dry streets of the city up the broad stairs that led from one story of her "mountain" to another. Cool breezes blew on her face and carried the scent of hundreds of blossoms. Soon she was high above the city, sitting under the shade of a tall tree, looking down at the gardens that her husband had made for her.

The mountain that Nebuchadnezzar made for his queen was called the Hanging Gardens of Babylon. It has completely disappeared and only the ruins of the foundation remain. We know about it from books that were written and from what archeologists have discovered, but some of its secrets are lost forever. Although it has gone, men have never forgotten what this engineer of Babylon was able to do.

4

A HOME FOR A GODDESS

Everyone knew what had fallen from the sky and what must be done about it.

It was many, many years ago in the town of Ephesus in the country of Greece. The Greeks believed that one of their gods, Jupiter, lived in the sky. Anything that fell from the heavens had been sent by him.

Greek towns were often dedicated to a certain god or goddess, and the patron of Ephesus was Diana. One day a strange black stone, shaped like a mummy, came hurtling down from above. We know from history that this was one of the many meteorites which fell at that time; but the people of Ephesus believed that it was a statue of Diana.

They built a temple at once, probably a very simple one, and put the meteorite in it. Before long

31

they built a larger temple, and through the years they rebuilt several times, each temple finer than the one before.

Some of the temples were destroyed in wars, and some of them were probably destroyed by the very ground on which they stood. It was a marshy place, too wet to support a heavy building, and some of them sank down into the ground. Others may have been ruined by earthquakes.

A time came when the town of Ephesus, which had become very wealthy, decided to build the most beautiful temple in the world for their goddess Diana, who had brought them such good fortune.

The Greeks had a special way of building, just as the Egyptians and Babylonians had. If you take a set of wooden building blocks you can build a solid, massive pyramid; if you use dominoes and stack them up to make walls you can imitate the brick buildings of the Babylonians. The Greeks used marble, which was harder and stronger than either granite or bricks. Their way of building is known as the post-and-lintel. Basically, this means two posts set upright, with a lintel, or beam, across the top.

A GREEK TEMPLE IN SICILY

If you will look at the nearest doorway, you will see that the two sides of the door might be called the posts; the top of the doorframe can be called the lintel. To make large temples, the Greeks had many posts set in the wall several feet apart. The walls were built solidly between the posts, and the roof was laid over the top of the lintels.

The Greeks loved the sun and air and wanted their buildings to be large but light and graceful. They were so beautiful that even today some of our buildings are made in the same way.

Greek temples were more beautiful than Egyptian pyramids or the brick buildings of the Babylonians. Everything about them was for a purpose, and no material was added that was not needed. Today this kind of design is called functional and it means that each part of the building is shaped for the job it has to do.

After the temples were completed many of the walls and posts were covered with beautifully colored sculpture, but the design of the building was always simple.

Post-and-lintel building presented a problem. The posts had to be set fairly close together. The distance between the posts was called the span— and the Greeks found that they could make no span wider than thirty feet. When posts were set farther apart than that, the lintel bent or broke.

They could have made large buildings with posts in the walls thirty feet apart, and others inside the building to hold up the roof, but this looked cluttered. Instead, they made the center of the temple with solid walls and a clear interior. Around this portion, they set rows of posts, and roofed over the entire structure. This made a very large temple which was almost all open to the sun and air.

The new Temple of Diana at Ephesus cost a great deal to build. When it was completed it was ranked with both the Pyramid of Cheops and the Hanging Gardens as a wonder of the world.

In the year 356 B.C. tragedy struck. A man named Herostratus wanted to do something so terrible that his name would never be forgotten. He shocked the world by destroying the temple.

The people of Ephesus began to rebuild at once. A great engineer, Theodoros of Samos, was called in for the job. He was called an architect because his main work was designing and building, but he was an engineer because of the problems he solved.

The first problem was the site of the temple. It would have been easier to put such a large structure on solid ground, but it was felt that Diana herself had selected this particular spot.

When the engineer looked at the ground where the temple was to be built, he saw that the top was filled with the remains of other temples. Each time one had been destroyed, it had been broken up into pieces and pounded into the ground, and the next one built on top. By this time there was quite a lot of broken stone and rubble on the site.

We do not know exactly how Theodoros made his foundation, except that he put down large masses of charcoal and sheepskins. We do know one kind of foundation that was used by people of his day in marshy places. Wooden piles, which were long poles, were charred on the outside to make them waterproof and driven into the ground closely together. The space between was covered with a layer of charcoal. Charcoal was used because it is light. A building on a foundation like this would be held into the ground by the piles, and supported by the charcoal.

For just a moment let us leave the Temple of Diana and make a quick trip to our own time. Some years ago, in Japan, an American architect was asked to build a large hotel. The man's name was Frank Lloyd Wright, and he faced the same problem as that faced by Theodoros. The hotel had to be built on marshy ground in an area where earthquakes were frequent. When Mr. Wright was shown the site, he saw that the ground had about eight feet of fairly hard soil over sixty feet of liquid mud.

He solved his problem by having pointed wooden piles, only eight feet long, driven into the ground, and then pulled out. Concrete was poured into the holes at once. Thousands of these short concrete posts were made as a foundation for the hotel. Mr. Wright said that they made a kind of giant pincushion on which the building rested.

The hotel "floated" on the liquid mud beneath the fairly solid ground—and when an earthquake came, the hotel moved back and forth but did not fall. It was the only building that stood unharmed through an earthquake that wrecked the whole city.

It seems that Theodoros must have done almost the same thing at the Temple of Diana. The ground underneath the temple, full of broken stone, made a kind of crust that floated on the marsh. If wooden piles were driven in through the crust, they would have been like the concrete posts used by Mr. Wright.

The other problem was to get the large marble columns from the stone quarry to the temple. The Greeks had wagons and carts for hauling, but the weight of the marble would have made the wheels sink into the marshy ground.

An engineer named Chersiphron was called in to help solve this problem. He would be called a consulting engineer today.

He had a long wooden framework made in which each marble column could turn like an axle. Oxen were hitched to the wooden frames, and as they pulled, the columns turned around and around, rolling over the ground. Thin wheels like those on wagons would have sunk into the ground, but the long columns did not. This seems like a very simple solution to the problem, but it made Cherisphron famous. Some of the most amazing things in the world seem simple after someone has thought of them.

When you look at a picture of a Greek temple,

OXEN WERE HITCHED TO THE WOODEN FRAME

you see that its tall marble columns seem to rise straight into the air. They are not exactly straight, but leaning slightly so that they will look straight. If you stand and look down a long, straight road, you notice that it seems to come to a point in the distance. The Greeks knew about this odd fact, so they slanted their columns to make them appear straight.

When the new Temple of Diana was finished, we are told that it was about 349 by 163 feet, and had one hundred marble columns, each eighty feet high. It was made of white marble, and most of the columns were carved in beautiful designs. We think of Greek buildings as being all white, but when they were new they were painted in brilliant colors.

The Temple of Diana was both beautiful and

wealthy. It was used both as a temple and as a bank, and kings and princes brought their riches there to be kept safely. People gave statues and paintings to the temple. A story is told about a painting of Alexander the Great. It showed him on horseback, and when it was finished he did not like it very much. Sometime later he came to look at it again, this time riding his horse. When the horse saw the painting it was startled, and whinnied. The artist laughed. "Your horse is a better judge of painting than you are," he said. "He thinks the picture is real."

For many centuries the Temple of Diana stood, the most famous temple in the world. It was finally destroyed, and builders used what was left for other things.

The temple is now almost entirely gone—but the ideas used by the engineers of ancient Greece are alive today.

5

THE ROADS THAT RULED THE WORLD

More than two thousand years ago the Roman people had safety pins, lending libraries, and furnaces. Even before the year 1, these people had ideas and skills much like ours. They were the first nation of engineers, and this helped them rule the world for many centuries.

Other countries had great engineers who did remarkable things, but the Romans used engineering to make their everyday lives better. Their cities had water systems which piped water to houses, buildings, parks, pools and public baths. They measured the amount of water used by each household, and sent bills for it, just as is done today.

The water systems were designed to bring large amounts of fresh water where it was needed, to lift it from one level to another, and to keep it clean as it flowed. Water will not flow uphill, so the Romans used something called the Archimedes' screw.

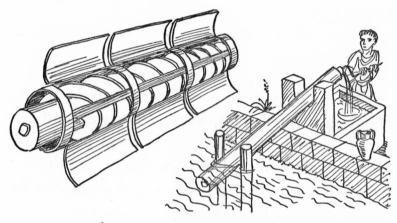

ARCHIMEDES' SCREW—A SECTION OF THE INTERIOR AND
THE SCREW BEING USED TO LIFT WATER

Think of a very large screw (similar to the small ones we use to fasten wood or metal together), with very wide thin ridges. This is fitted tightly into a round tube with a handle to turn the screw coming out of one end. The open bottom end of the screw is set into a pool of water, and as the handle is turned the water enters the tube between the ridges. As the screw is turned, the water flows around the ridges to the top, and finally flows out the open end. This is another kind of inclined plane, used to move something from one place to another. Other countries had used the Archimedes' screw before the Romans had, but probably not so successfully.

Water was cleaned on its way to the city by settling ponds. These were pools dug along the flow of water and dammed almost to the top. They slowed down the flow of water so that dirt or gravel carried in it would sink to the bottom.

Most Roman cities had large public baths which were much like our public swimming pools of today. One bathhouse often had many different pools with water of different temperatures. Water for the pools was heated in the basement of the buildings and carried through pipes up to the bathing rooms. Probably Archimedes' screws were used for this, and the hot water was mixed with cold to make each bath a different temperature.

The Romans even had doors that shut by themselves. We have doors today that are closed by electric eyes or air pressure devices, but the Romans simply hung their doors on a slant. After someone had pushed them open and walked through, they swung back into place.

In almost everything they did, the Romans used what we call know-how. They decided what they wanted to do, thought about what they had to work with, and found a way to make what they had do the job.

Most of their large buildings were made of stone and concrete. They knew, as the Egyptians and Greeks had known, that stone was long-lasting, and they also knew its drawbacks.

One reason stone is so strong is that it is so heavy. The heavier anything is, the more it is pulled downward toward the earth by gravity. Strange as it seems, the pull of gravity on a solid stone building makes it strong.

The pyramids are a good example of this. One large stone block is heavy and difficult to move. If layer after layer of stone blocks are piled on top of each other, the weight is so great that almost nothing can knock them down. A stone laid flat on the ground, or flat on top of a solid foundation, is being pulled by gravity over its entire surface. Stone used in this way is said to be in compression.

When the Greeks used the post-and-lintel way of building, gravity caused a problem. The tall heavy columns with their bottom ends resting flat on the earth were more or less in compression and were pulled upon evenly by gravity. The stone lintel or beam that lay across them was also pulled on by gravity, but the part between the posts was being pulled toward the earth. Stone supported only on each end and stretching across space is called in flexure and is weakened by this pull of gravity.

The Romans did not want solid stone buildings like the pyramids, nor did they want the problem of post-and-lintel building. They wanted *all* of their stone in compression—and they discovered the secret of the arch.

An arch is like a doorway with a curved top. Other nations had used it, but not as the Romans did.

If you draw a circle and another smaller circle inside of it, you have the beginning of an arch. Draw a line across the center of the two circles, and the top half is the ring of the arch.

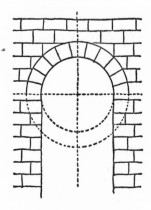

.A ROMAN ARCH

The Romans may have drawn just such a pattern before beginning an arch. At the very top they drew two slanting lines which made a section like a piece of pie with the tip cut off. The rest of the ring was divided by more slanting lines which showed them the way to cut separate stones.

A wooden framework was set up where the arch was to be, with the outside cut to exactly the size and shape of the inner circle of the ring of the arch. On each side of this, strong solid supports, or posts, were built. The first stones of the arch were put on each support, then the next, and then the next.

THE ROMANS USED THE ARCH IN BUILDING THIS AQUEDUCT

At last the pie-shaped piece, or keystone, was put in place. It fit very tightly, and the force of gravity pulling on it held the entire arch in place. Since the stones were fitted together at a slant, they could not slip out of position. The stronger the pull of gravity, the more tightly they were pulled together. The thrust of the arch, or force of the pull, was carried down through the arch to its supports, and then to the ground. The arch could not fall unless the supports were moved out—and they were made so heavy and strong that they did not move.

The Roman arch was half as high as it was wide, which meant that the buildings were rather low, with wide columns to support the arches. They were a big step forward in the long struggle of man to use the materials of the world to fit his needs. Some of them are still standing today, as monuments to their makers.

Another kind of arch, called the barrel vault, was also used by the Romans. Just as a roller is a long wheel, so the barrel vault is a long arch—one that has depth as well as width and height. Barrel vaults were used as roofs for churches, for roofs of underground water systems, and even for the roof of the great Roman sewage system, the Cloaca Maxima.

It is not surprising that people as clever as the

Romans became very powerful. They used their engineering skill in their homes and cities, and also in wars with other countries. The time came when Rome ruled almost the entire world, with an empire that reached from deep into Africa far up into what are now the British Isles.

A BARREL VAULT IN A ROMAN BATH AT POMPEII

The Roman army was strong enough to defeat almost any other army, but it was not large enough to stay in every defeated country and rule. How could this huge empire be held together and ruled from one city in the southern part of Europe?

The engineers of Rome solved this problem. For the first time in the history of the world, a giant system of highways was built. These roads stretched for fifty thousand miles, linking every part of the empire with Rome.

The routes they were to take were chosen with great care to make them as straight as possible. This job was done so well that many modern European roads follow the same paths.

They reached out from Rome like the spokes of a giant wheel, making it possible for Roman soldiers to travel rapidly wherever they were needed. It is said that a horse-drawn cart could go sixty or seventy miles a day on them, a speed record which must have amazed everyone.

If you have ever watched men build a highway, you will be interested in how the Romans made theirs so long ago.

After the route was chosen, furrows were ploughed on each side of the ground where the road was to be, from sixteen to thirty-two feet apart. Trenches were dug in the furrows to find out what kind of soil lay beneath. Highways, as well as buildings, need good foundations.

Often the entire roadway was dug out until solid ground was reached. This was done by hand, with picks and shovels, and the earth was carried away in baskets. If the diggers did not reach a solid foundation, they had to make one. Wooden piles were driven into the ground, very close together, and on these a kind of mattress made of timber and rushes was laid.

Once the foundation was ready, the road itself was built in layers. Often the bottom one was a heavy coating of sand, which would fill in rough spots and make a smooth surface. Over this was put a layer of small stones, with larger ones on the outside edges. These outside stones were built high to make a short retaining wall. Over this layer was put a coat of concrete, then another layer of sand or gravel concrete. This layer was curved higher in the center so that rain or melted snow could drain off. Because of the speed of our traffic, our highways today must be level, which means that water tends to stand on them and do damage. Small Roman carts could travel well on a slightly curved road. When our traffic, a generation or so ago, was mostly horse-drawn, our own roads were graded much like the Roman highways.

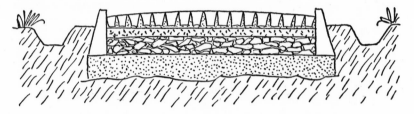

THE LAYERS THAT MADE A ROMAN ROAD

While the top layer of concrete was still wet and soft, carefully cut and finished stones were set in it to make a hard, durable surface. The finished road was from two and one-half to five feet thick. It was so strong and massive that it has been said "the Roman roads were like walls lying on their sides."

Perhaps few of our modern highways are as rugged and well built as were these that were made so long ago. They were made to hold one vast empire together, and to last as long as they were needed.

6

THE BRIDGE THAT WON A WAR

A great Roman general built one of the most famous bridges in history, and won a war by doing it.

Julius Caesar was leading his army into a country where a wild and savage people lived. One day his advance scouts brought word that a large swift river would have to be crossed. The enemy lay in wait on the other side.

Caesar's men could not wade through the river, and small boats would have been dangerous. The current was so strong that only a bridge would solve the problem.

It was much easier for Caesar to decide he wanted a bridge than it was to build one in this particular spot.

The simplest bridge is a log laid across a stream

from bank to bank—but no log would do here. The Romans often built boat bridges, and carried the materials with them on fighting expeditions. When they built this kind of bridge a row of boats was put side by side across a river, with heavy anchors to hold them in place. Two strong cables of rope were stretched across the river above the boats and pulled tight by windlasses. This was the foundation. Timber was laid solidly crosswise on the cables, and a brushwood mattress piled on top. Dirt was put over the brush and stamped down— a kind of road across a river. Sometimes fences were built on each side so that horses, crossing the bridge, could not see the water beneath them and be frightened. Boat bridges worked across placid rivers, but not in a current as fierce as this.

The Romans built wonderful solid bridges of stone blocks and concrete. They were supported by rows of arches that stood, strong and sturdy, against the current. The arches were often so heavy, and the space between them so narrow, that they took up most of the river bed. This made the level of the river rise higher, so that the bridge had

A ROMAN STONE BRIDGE

to be built very tall to keep well above water.

Of course such a bridge could not be built here. This was the Rhine River in Germany.

Caesar was the sort of engineer who liked problems. He decided to use the force of the river to make his bridge stronger.

He put his men to work cutting huge timbers, eighteen inches in diameter, with one end sharpened to a point. These were measured to fit the depth of the river.

These timbers were fastened together in pairs with crosspieces every two feet which made them look like ladders.

When the first set of timbers was ready, it was floated out onto the river by men on rafts. A little way from the bank the pointed ends of the timbers were lowered into the river, slanted against the current. They were hammered down until the ends set firmly into the bed of the river. Another pair and still another was taken out and set in place until the row reached across the river. The swift current did not dislodge them because they were hammered in so securely, and also because they leaned against the current.

As soon as this row was completed, another row was set parallel to it, forty feet downstream, leaning against the current. Each pair of joined timbers, called balks, was now matched by another pair just across from it.

Each pair of balks was now joined to its mate by a huge timber, called a transom, which fitted tightly into the top open space. These transoms were braced by crosspieces set on the outside of each pair of balks, which held them in place and kept the balks apart.

Now the bridge was so made that the very force

CAESAR'S BRIDGE ACROSS THE RHINE

of the water made it stronger. The harder the water pushed on it, the tighter it held together.

To make the bridge more secure, very long poles with pointed ends were cut and fastened to the end of each transom. The pointed end was set at an angle to the current into the stream and hammered into the bed of the river. The force of the river against the transom pushed this extra support deeper into place, making the bridge even stronger. These poles were called buttresses. Another set was made above the bridge, slanting against the current. This set was to act as a bumper, in case the enemy thought of floating tree trunks downstream to break the bridge.

Long logs were laid across the transoms, making a floor for the bridge which stretched from one side of the river to the other. Brush and short poles were laid on top of this, and Caesar had completed his bridge.

It had taken him ten days to do something that everyone would have agreed was impossible. Now his army would not have to take small boats across the swift current. They could march proudly across a sturdy bridge. Every man in Caesar's army must have been proud to be a Roman as he made his way to meet the enemy.

When they reached the other side of the river,

they found that they had done even more than they knew. The enemy did not want to fight such an army, but was ready to surrender.

They knew how fierce the Rhine was, and had probably not dreamed that anyone could bridge it. When they saw these strange soldiers do such a wonderful job in such a short time they decided it was no use trying to fight an army that could work miracles.

The bridge that had defeated a mighty river had also defeated the enemy.

7

BUILDINGS WITH WINGS

There came a time when the world forgot the skills it had learned.

The Roman Empire, which had been so powerful, collapsed. Fierce, warlike people called barbarians came into Europe from Asia and people had little time for anything but fighting. Life was hard, and the barbarians did not bring new skills and ideas to take the place of those that were gone.

Only in the monasteries was knowledge treasured and kept alive. They were religious centers, and a refuge for scholars and artists. These people remembered and wrote about the past.

Almost the only large buildings put up in this time were churches. There had always been problems man could not solve about large buildings.

The Greeks had not been able to make long

spans, so their temples had rows of columns not more than thirty feet apart. The Roman arch was strong and could span a longer distance, but the columns of the arch had to be heavy and solid to support the weight. Churches were sometimes built with a barrel vault roof, but the walls below it had to be almost solid.

An attractive building could be made by using four arches set in a square, one arch to a side, but how could the roof be put on? A dome, which looked like half of a ball, was the roof most liked, but it could not sit securely on the tops of the arches. Several ways to fill the empty spaces left between a round roof on a square building were tried, but none of them worked very well.

When the Emperor Justinian came to the throne, he wanted a very special church built. He called in two architects from near Ephesus, which had been the center of new ideas in building since the time of the great Temple of Diana.

These men, Anthemius and Isodorus, invented something called a "dome on pendentives." The pendentive was the answer to the problem of fitting a round roof to a square building. It was a spherical triangle which fitted into the empty space between the tops of the arches and the dome. Like many other inventions, it seemed quite simple—once someone had thought of it.

The church built by Anthemius and Isodorus had a great central square with sides about one hundred and twenty feet long. At each corner, to support the arches, was a column a hundred feet high. The

THE DOME WAS ONE HUNDRED AND TWENTY FEET ACROSS

arches which connected the corners were sixty feet high. If you remember that the longest span the Greeks could make was thirty feet, you will see that this was a big advance. The dome that crowned this huge building was one hundred and twenty feet across and forty-six feet high.

A man who wrote about it said, "In height it rises to the very heavens and overtops neighboring buildings like a ship anchored among them." Another man said that the dome "does not appear to rest on a solid foundation, but to cover the space beneath as though it were suspended from heaven."

Man had come a long way since the pyramids.

Justinian's church was St. Sophia's at Constantinople, and it was built more than two thousand years ago. Justinian died in the year 565 and it was not until the Middle Ages that men again wished to build large and beautiful churches. The Dark Ages were losing their hold on Europe and new hopes and ideas began to spread. Religion became stronger than it had ever been, and with it came the urge to raise temples that seemed to soar to the sky.

INSIDE ST. SOPHIA IN CONSTANTINOPLE

When people make up their minds to do something, it often seems that the things they need are ready for them. New ideas that made the great cathedrals of Europe possible could now be used. Travelers to the East had seen pointed arches. These arches were used mainly for decoration, but engineers saw a way to make them practical.

In the low, wide arch of the Romans, the pull of gravity was exerted on the entire span. This made a very strong thrust, or push, against the support. Since a pointed arch had much less span it did not have to be twice as wide as it was high, and could have much smaller supports. Since it had a fairly short span, it could be of any height wished.

For many centuries men had known that every building has a downward thrust. If you pile a stack of blocks too high, it will fall over, and buildings will do the same unless they are designed right. One way to avoid this is to make the walls strong and heavy, and prop them up with a buttress. Caesar used buttresses on his Rhine bridge, but the ones used for buildings were so thick they made walls look even heavier. An early buttress was a

Right: AN EARLY SOLID BUTTRESS
Left: A FLYING BUTTRESS

solid piece of stone or masonry that jutted out from a wall to the ground.

During the Middle Ages, the flying buttress was invented. This was a kind of half-arch with one end resting on the ground and the other resting against the foot of an arch which was supported by a column. The downward thrust of the arch was carried through the slender flying buttress to the ground and held the column secure.

Using these two ideas, the pointed arch and the flying buttress, engineers of the Middle Ages made tall beautiful cathedrals filled with light and air. Some of them are still standing today. If you visit one of them, or see one in our country built in the same manner, you will find both of these ideas at work.

In the years between 1220 and 1288, the cathedral at Amiens was made. A historian said, "whenever the great blocks of stone were hauled up by cable from the quarry, the people of the district, and even those of neighboring regions, nobles and commoners alike, harnessed themselves to the ropes by arms, breasts and shoulders, and drew the load like beasts of burden."

The finished cathedral rose to three hundred sixty feet, or about the height of a modern thirty-story building. The central part was four hundred seventy feet long and only forty-six feet wide. To those standing inside it, the stone roof was so far above that it seemed to be looked at from a distance. The roof appeared like a great sail stretched over the ribs of the vault, and held up by a continuous wind from below. The giant flying buttresses on the outside, which helped support the walls, seemed to leap upward from the ground.

BUILDING A CATHEDRAL

Like the builders of the pyramids, the engineers who helped make the cathedrals were working in stone—but man had learned to make stone do what he wished. The pyramids were heavy, solid, and massive—the cathedrals were so light, graceful and airy that they seemed to be "music frozen into stone." Some of them still stand today, to remind us that when man's dreams soar to the sky, he can make them come true.

8

THE LIGHT THAT SAVED
A MILLION LIVES

The trouble with lighthouses is that it is almost impossible to build them where they are needed.

Large ships are more in danger close to land than in the open sea. Near the coast there are often dangerous currents and sharp rocks that cannot be seen at night. The more dangerous a coast is, the more a lighthouse is needed—and the harder it is to build one.

In the English Channel, near Plymouth Harbor, is a group of rocks called the Eddystone Rocks. At high tide they can barely be seen, but at low tide wicked, sharp, dismal ridges of stone rise above the water. During storms and in the winter a ship that chances near them will probably be wrecked. When the wind blows from the southwest, as it often does, a ship that happens to be close may be pounded to bits by the rushing waters, which seem to go in every direction at once.

Ships coming through the channel long ago knew about the terrible Eddystone Rocks and took a course as far away from them as possible. Unfortunately, this meant that they sailed close to the French coast, which was almost as dangerous, and many of them were wrecked there. Something had to be done—and only great engineering skill could solve the problem. How could a lighthouse be built on such a wild spot, especially when the weather and tides made work impossible most of the year?

In the middle of the eighteenth century, an Englishman named John Smeaton was given the job. He was not known as an engineer, but as a man who made mathematical instruments.

All of his life he had been interested in making things, and this presented quite a problem to his father. In those days in England, men who worked with their hands were not considered gentlemen. In spite of this, young John spent most of his time with his tools and inventions. When he was four-

teen he created a family crisis. He carefully built
a forcing pump and tried it out on his father's fish
pond. It was entirely successful—the pond was
soon completely empty of both water and fish.
John was probably happy to see how well his pump
worked, but his father must have wondered what
he was going to do with his problem son.

When John was 32, he was asked to take on the
job of building a lighthouse on the Eddystone
Rocks. Two other lighthouses had been built there,
neither of which had lasted. John knew all about
them, and knew that he had to do a better job.

The first one had been built by an odd person
named Henry Winstanley. Mr. Winstanley's house
was full of strange inventions. If you had visited
him and seen a slipper lying on the floor, it would
have been wise not to kick it. If you had, a ghost
might have risen up before you. If anyone sat on
a certain chair, it suddenly flung out its arms and
held him tight.

It isn't surprising that a man like Winstanley
built a very strange lighthouse. Work was begun
in the summer, because only then could a boat get

to the rocks. Even then there were weeks when work had to be stopped. During a storm, waves three hundred feet high lashed the site and buried everything beneath them.

Mr. Winstanley had deep holes drilled in the rock and iron rods sunk in them. These were to hold the foundation of the lighthouse. A round pillar twelve feet high, made of solid stone, was fastened to the rock by means of the iron rods, and the lighthouse itself was built on top of that.

It looked like a Chinese pagoda with open galleries and projections on all sides. The gallery around the lantern was so wide that a six-oared ship could be driven through it by the waves when seas ran high.

Structures that will be beaten upon by wind and sea should be designed to offer the least possible resistance. This is what we mean when we talk of stream-line design—a shape that will cut through air and water instead of opposing it. Mr. Winstanley's lighthouse had far too many things sticking out to catch the force of wind and wave to be practical.

Mr. Winstanley admired his design. He boasted of how strong his lighthouse was, and said that he would like to stay in it through the worst storm that ever visited the earth. Unfortunately, his wish was granted. In November of 1703, Mr. Winstanley and some workmen were in it making repairs. A terrible storm arose—one of the worst ever seen in that area. During the night of the twenty-sixth, people of Plymouth wondered, as they heard the fury of the wind and waves, what was happening. In the morning they looked toward the Eddystone Rocks, and saw nothing—the entire lighthouse, with everyone in it, had been completely washed away.

It was three years before anyone was ready to try to build again on this dangerous spot. This time a man named John Rudyard, who was a silk mercer, was chosen for the job. His design for the lighthouse was quite simple—a smooth round column which would offer the least possible resistance to wind and wave.

The Rudyard lighthouse was partly timber and partly stone. The bottom two layers were stout

Left: MR. WINSTANLEY'S LIGHTHOUSE
Right: JOHN RUDYARD'S DESIGN

oak, bolted into Eddystone Rocks. On top of these were five layers of heavy Cornish granite, then more oak. Mr. Rudyard knew that weight meant strength in a building.

The lighthouse itself was built on top of this solid foundation, and made mostly of timber. It was completed in 1709. While it was being built England and France were at war. There is a story that a French ship captured and carried off some of the men who were working on the Eddystone Light. When the king of France found out who the prisoners were, he ordered that they be returned at once, and sent gifts with them. He said that he was at war with England, but not with mankind.

For forty-six years Rudyard's lighthouse stood, and threw a beam that kept ships from being dashed to pieces on the terrible rocks. On December 2, 1755, disaster struck this second lighthouse. Fire broke out and the entire structure was destroyed. The three men in it were saved from the flames by hiding in a cave on one side of the rock. One of them, however, was the victim of a peculiar accident. While throwing water on the cupola at the top of the lighthouse, during the fire, he was hit on the head and shoulders by melted lead.

The doctor who treated him for his burns could not understand why he did not recover. The man insisted that he had swallowed some of the melted lead, but the doctor could not believe it. After the workman's death, a flat oval piece of lead was discovered in his stomach.

This was the history of the Eddystone lighthouses when John Smeaton was asked to put up another one. He was perfectly sure that he could do it, though he had never tackled such a job before.

Engineers learn from the past, as all of us do, and Mr. Smeaton knew that the heavier a building is, the more strongly the force of gravity will hold it in place. He said that he was going to build a lighthouse so solid that the sea would give way to it, not it to the sea. He chose as the model for his design the trunk of a sturdy oak tree—smooth and cylindrical, but slightly smaller at the top than at the bottom.

His plan was to use stone, but the man who had hired him objected. The lighthouse was needed as

soon as possible, and they were sure a timber building could be put up faster. Mr. Smeaton did not let
a little problem like this bother him. The timber
lighthouse of Mr. Rudyard had been put up in four
years, so he promised to put up a stone one in the
same length of time.

He had to make every minute count, and to invent ways of getting things done efficiently.

He decided to have the stone cut and fitted on
the mainland. This was especially important since
bad weather made working time at the site short.
While the stone was being prepared, he had the
foundation begun at Eddystone.

Every minute of good weather had to be used,
since he never knew from one day to another what
the weather would be. A workboat was kept anchored a quarter of a mile from Eddystone, so that
men and materials could be brought in quickly
when it was possible to work. When the other
lighthouses were being built, no one had thought
of this, so everything had been kept at Plymouth,
fourteen miles away.

The foundation was to be the most massive, and

heaviest, ever built on the site. Parts of the Eddystone Rocks themselves were used, and other huge stones were locked into them by dovetailing. Matching slots and projections were made on stones to be fitted together, and they were put in place like a huge jigsaw puzzle. To make the foundation even more secure, Mr. Smeaton had channels cut between stones, and wooden wedges pounded into them, then set with mortar. These wedges were set so as to make every stone push even more tightly against the others. The harder the sea lashed at such a foundation, the more tightly it held.

To fasten the next layer of stone on top of the foundation, plugs of marble were used. Holes a foot square were drilled in the foundation, and matching holes were drilled in the stones which would be on top. Plugs of solid marble were fitted into these holes and fastened securely with mortar. The only way one layer of foundation could be broken from another was by a force strong enough to break these marble plugs in two.

When the foundation was built high enough to

be like a flat platform, Mr. Smeaton was delighted. He climbed to the top and accidentally lost his footing. He slipped and fell onto the sharp rocks

BUILDING THE LIGHTHOUSE

below. The tide was out, so his only injury was a dislocated thumb. Since there was no doctor available, Mr. Smeaton promptly set his own thumb, and got back to work.

At the end of September the weather became so bad that no more work could be done. The men took their tools and returned to the mainland. On the 12th of May they returned, anxious to see what the terrible winter had done to their work. To their delight, they found that the foundation was exactly as they had left it. The mortar had set firmly, and the stones were as solid as the Eddystone Rocks themselves.

The completed lighthouse was ready for use in August, 1759, three years after it was started. It had taken Mr. Smeaton a year less to build a stone lighthouse than it had taken Mr. Rudyard to build a timber one.

For more than a hundred years it stood, strong and stalwart, throwing a light-saving beam across the stormy waters. There was only one drawback—the huge waves which struck the lighthouse were carried up the smooth curved face until they reached the bottom of the lantern gallery. Then they were broken up by the cornice and made a heavy spray which covered the lantern for a moment. Their force was so great that they lifted the rocks of the cornice up in the air.

The lighthouse was so well built that it lasted in

spite of this and was repaired and strengthened only twice.

After it had stood and served mankind for more than a century, the rocks on which it was built became undermined by action of the sea.

Mr. Smeaton had made a lighthouse that had not been broken by the seas, but had broken them—and the Eddystone Rocks themselves gave way before it did.

9

A ROAD BENEATH A RIVER

Engineers learn things in strange places, and from strange things. One of the world's best engineers learned from a worm.

Marc Isambard Brunel was working on a job in England at the Chatham Dockyard. He became interested in a small worm, about four inches long, which was not really a worm at all, but a shellfish called a teredo or shipworm. The teredo makes tunnels through timbers used to support piers and docks—countless tiny tunnels which eventually weaken the timbers so that they have to be replaced.

Mr. Brunel was interested in how such a tiny worm did so much destructive work. Covering its head is a shell with two rows of teeth-like edges.

This shell protects the body of the teredo and helps it cut tunnels through heavy wood.

Sometime after Mr. Brunel had watched the teredo at work he was given the job of digging a tunnel under the Thames River in London. The lesson he had learned from a worm helped him invent a machine which made it possible for men to dig tunnels all over the world.

Men have been digging holes in the ground since the beginning of history. Some of these holes were tunnels, and this is one of the hardest, and most dangerous, of all kinds of engineering. In early days, men dug tunnels with hand tools through solid rock. Digging through rock is slow, difficult work, but such a tunnel is permanent once it is finished. Digging in the ground itself is much more dangerous, since the walls and ceiling are apt to slide and fall down as fast as they are dug.

In the eighteenth century in England, a group of people decided that it would be a good idea to dig a tunnel under the river Thames. It was taking longer and longer to cross the river, which was crowded with boats, and the tunnel would make a road under it. Someone tried to dig the tunnel, but failed completely. The idea was forgotten for five years until Richard Trevithick decided to try again. He dug a huge hole, eleven feet wide, about one hundred yards from the bank of the river. This was called a "heading" and was to lead down to the opening of the proposed tunnel. Water filled this shaft as fast as it was dug and had to be pumped out continually. When it had gone down forty feet the hole was made narrower—only eight feet wide—until it was seventy-six feet deep. The work was done with picks and shovels and the water was pumped out by hand. The soil dug out was lifted in baskets hung on hand pulleys.

At the bottom of the shaft a tunnel under the river was started. This was only thirty inches wide at the top and three feet wide at the bottom, and five feet high. Of course Mr. Trevithick planned to make it larger before he finished.

The work was hard and dangerous. The bed of the river was twenty-five to thirty feet above the top of the tunnel, but the weight of the river itself was added to the weight of the soil. Twice high tides in the river made the weight of the water so great that the tunnel collapsed. The story of what finally destroyed the tunnel may or may not be true, but it is interesting. It is said that Mr. Trevithick overheard someone say that the tunnel was not being dug in a straight line. This made him angry and he decided to prove that he was doing a good job. He had a man row to the spot in the river just above the spot where the center of the tunnel was supposed to be, and wait there. With some of his workmen, he went into the tunnel and began pushing long jointed rods up through the roof until the ends reached above the surface of the water. He believed that when all of the rods were in place they would make a straight line which would end just where the man waited in the boat.

Unfortunately, pushing rods through the roof let the Thames break through. Mr. Trevithick and the other men had to run for their lives. After that, leading engineers agreed that it was impossible to dig a tunnel under the Thames.

Fifteen years later Mr. Brunel had a plan which he knew would work. He had made a huge shell with sharp cutting edges which he called a shield. The shell had twelve frames, each twenty-two feet high and three feet broad. Every frame was di-

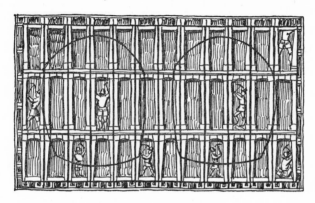

MR. BRUNEL'S SHIELD

vided into three compartments, each large enough for a man to stand in and work. It was something like a huge cookie cutter which could be pushed through the heavy blue clay under the Thames. Men standing in the frames could shovel out the loosened earth, and pass it back under the shell from where it could be carried out. The heavy iron frame would support the roof and sides of the tunnel as it was being dug. Men in the back part

of the shield could set brick roof, sides and floor
to hold the tunnel.

The shield was like the shell of the teredo, pro-
tecting the men as they dug, and holding the tunnel
safe until it could be lined with brick.

Giant screw jacks were placed with one end
against the finished brickwork and the other end
against the back of the cutting edges of the shield
to push it forward as the work progressed. These
screw jacks were a kind of inclined plane. The
Egyptians built a very long inclined plane to raise
stones a fairly short way into the air. A road wind-
ing round and round a mountain may be many
times as long as the mountain is high, but it is an
easy way of getting to the top.

The screw jack is an inclined plane which works
differently—a weight is not moved over it, but it
moves under the weight!

The threads of the screw are the inclined plane,
going round and round the screw. The screw is
turned by a handle set in the end. When the handle
is turned, the inclined plane of the threads go
round. The handle turns much farther than the

threads of the screw—it must go in a complete circle to raise a weight as far as the distance between two of the threads.

An automobile jack works in the same way, and makes it possible for a man to lift a two- or three-ton car up into the air.

The screw jacks in the Brunel shield were laid on their side, so the handle could be turned only in half a circle. It took three and one half tons of pressure to push each foot of cutting edge of the shield through the clay of the tunnel, and the screw jacks made this possible.

One of the dangers of the shield was that the great cuts of earth made by each section might fall in and crush the workmen. To avoid this, Mr. Brunel made plank coverings in front of each section. The top plank could be removed, the loose earth dug out, and the plank replaced. Then the next plank was removed, and the process repeated. In this way, only a small portion of the clay was uncovered at a time so the workmen were safe.

When the tunnel was dug so far that it ran into ground as wet as thin mud, the wooden shield was changed to work like a venetian blind. Even smaller sections could be opened, and the rest held in place.

Even with the great shield, work in the tunnel was dangerous and the workmen were nervous. They were doing what man had never done before, and no one knew what might happen. When they had dug quite a long way under the Thames they became so frightened they quit. More men had to be found before the work could go on, but Mr. Brunel was not discouraged.

Several times the river broke into the tunnel and work had to be stopped until it could be pumped dry. Mr. Brunel had to strengthen the very bed of the river in order to make it safer. Boats were loaded with bags of clay fastened to four-foot-long sticks, and these were dropped into the weak places in the bed of the river. The bags of clay would sink to the bottom, the bags would hold the clay in place, and the sticks would hold the bags in place. Tons of gravel were poured in on top of the bags.

On one terrible day when the tunnel was six

hundred feet long, and success seemed in sight, it flooded again. The men worked heroically, but it was no use. Tons of raging water swept through, and everyone had to flee before it.

This time Mr. Brunel had four thousand tons of soil dumped into the river bed, and the tunnel was pumped out again. The brickwork was not damaged, but the great shield was broken. So much money had already been spent that everyone lost faith in the tunnel, except Mr. Brunel. For seven years it was abandoned, and no more work was done.

By 1836 Mr. Brunel had a new and stronger shield built, and his backers had been persuaded to let him try again. Over and over the work was hampered by water and weakened earth. Then a new danger appeared. In digging, the men sometimes struck pockets of gas in the earth, and fell unconscious as they worked. The soil itself became so wet that the top compartments of the shield had to be closed until a way could be found to make them waterproof.

In spite of all this, Mr. Brunel persisted. By

March in 1841, everyone was sure that the tunnel
would be finished, and Mr. Brunel was given honors
by the Queen of England. That August, he was
able to walk through the tunnel from one side of
the river to the other. Finally it was completed,
just as he planned it.

One of the strangest parts of the story of the
great tunnel under the Thames is that people got
tired of it. For a while they were glad to pay a
small fee for the privilege of taking this short cut

A CROSS SECTION OF THE THAMES TUNNEL

under the river, but then they stopped. It was no longer something new and interesting to do.

In 1865, the tunnel was sold to the East London Railway for less than half of what it had cost to build. Underground railroads took the place of foot traffic.

It might seem that in spite of all the courage and persistence and skill that it took to build, the tunnel under the Thames was a failure. It was not a failure, but a beginning.

The great shield, suggested by a tiny worm, had conquered a new field in engineering. More and better ones were built, and man was able to make tunnels where and when he wanted them.

10

VOICES UNDER THE SEA

Some men don't know when they have failed. When others are ready to give up, they keep on working at what they started to do, and continue until they have succeeded.

Charles T. Bright, an English engineer, wanted to do something no one had ever done before. An American, Cyrus W. Field, agreed with him that people could talk to each other across the Atlantic Ocean.

Almost everyone else in the world thought that they were wrong. It was true that Samuel Morse, in America, had invented the telegraph, which used electricity to carry messages through wire. The new invention worked well on top of the ground—but under water was something else again. Telegraph wire could be made into a cable for underwater use by coating it or putting it inside a metal tube. Mr. Morse had laid such a short cable in New York harbor which worked for a few hours. Then a ship, raising its anchor, caught the cable and destroyed two hundred feet of it. Another short cable had been laid for twenty-five miles between England and France. It lasted only long enough to send a few words. Right in the middle of the first message a fisherman hooked on to the line and dragged it to the surface, thinking it was a new kind of seaweed.

These experiments were interesting, but few people took them seriously. Even if a short cable could be laid (and not hauled up by mistake), it was certainly impossible to lay a wire almost two thousand miles long on the bottom of the ocean.

Scientists said that the ocean was too deep for a cable to sink to the bottom. They believed that it would sink just so far, and then, because of the weight of the water above and below, would float. These men believed that gold and treasure from wrecked ships never reached the bed of the ocean, but were floating far beneath the surface.

Other scientists did not believe that telegraph messages could travel such a great distance. They said that the electrical impulses which were sent along the wire could not be made strong enough to go from England to America.

People who were not scientists had even odder ideas. Some believed that Mr. Bright intended to send messages by jerking one end of the cable so it could be felt on the other. One man, who saw a small piece of the kind of cable Mr. Bright meant to use, said, "Oh! Now I know how you can store it aboard the ship. You cut it up into bits beforehand, and then join up the pieces as you lay."

Mr. Bright and Mr. Field had another friend, John Brett, who had helped with the cable between France and England. The three of them knew they could do the job. Mr. Bright and Mr. Brett had the engineering skill, and Mr. Field had a genius for raising money. They were ready to begin.

Unlike other engineers who could learn from those who worked in the past, these men had to learn as they worked. Never, in the history of the world, had anyone attempted to do what they planned.

Just about this time two things which would be a great help to them happened. One of them was the discovery of gutta-percha, a rubbery substance made from the juice of the gutta-percha tree. It is very strong and flexible, can be shaped in any way desired, and is waterproof. It was exactly what was needed to coat the wires of a submarine cable. A machine was invented to coat wires with gutta-percha, and a step toward the big cable was taken.

In 1856 American and English scientists studied the bed of the ocean. They found what seemed a place designed by nature for a cable.

They used a clever sounding rod—a thin iron rod, hollow at the lower end. A heavy "cannon-ball" weight was attached to this by two links which were held down by the weight of the ball. When the end of the iron rod touched the bottom of the ocean, the ball rested on the bottom and no longer pulled on the links. The cannon ball was thus released and stayed on the bottom while the thin iron rod was pulled to the top. Inside the hollow end of the rod were clues to tell the scientists what the bed of the ocean was like.

The clues were shells so tiny they had to be

studied under a microscope. They were found to be almost all perfect and not surrounded by sand or gravel. This meant that the ocean bed was quiet, with no strong currents. If it had been rough or pushed about by heavy currents, the small shells would have been broken and damaged. This proved that there was a soft bed of thin mud all along one section of the route from England to America. To Mr. Bright this seemed a perfect feather bed, waiting for a cable to be laid on it. The scientist who reported on the exploration did not agree. He said that he was sure no one would ever find "a time calm enough, the sea smooth enough, a wire long enough, or a ship big enough, to lay a coil of wire one thousand six hundred miles in length."

At this moment, Mr. Bright was not interested in his opinion. The cable was already being made. The American and English governments had each promised the use of a ship for laying the cable. In exchange their official messages were to be sent free once the cable was working.

Mr. Bright disagreed with the scientists who said

that a cable would not sink to the bottom of the ocean, and that an electrical impulse could not be sent so far. He believed that as the cable sank deeper into the water, the increased weight on it would compress it, or make it smaller. This meant that it would weigh more as it was more compressed, and would keep on sinking—and since it would be very tightly compressed at such a depth, it would be an even better and more waterproof cable.

No one knew for sure whether or not an electrical impulse could be sent for more than two thousand miles over a wire. Light impulses could be sent for short distances, and the electricians planned to send a heavy charge to travel the greater distance.

Mr. Bright was concerned because the cable was not being made as he wished. He thought it should be heavier, and the insulation should be thicker. No one else agreed with him. Electricians said that a larger cable would require more electricity. The men raising money for the project said that a larger cable would cost so much more it would not be worth while. It would also take longer to make, and they wanted to finish it and get it laid as soon as possible.

The finished cable weighed one ton for each nautical mile and would stand a strain of more than three tons without breaking. In the center were seven strands of small copper wires twisted together and insulated with three coats of guttapercha. This was wrapped in hemp saturated with pitch, oil, tar and wax. A sheath of 126 iron cables was wrapped spirally around this, and then the cable was drawn through a tar mixture. It was planned to start laying the cable from Valentia on the west coast of Ireland across to Trinity Bay on the east coast of Newfoundland.

Two ships, the English *Agamemnon* and the American *Niagara,* were to sail from Valentia side by side until they reached the middle of the ocean. Cable was to be laid from the *Niagara* first. When the mid-point of the route was reached the ends of the cable were to be spliced, and the *Agamemnon* would continue laying it until it reached the other shore.

LAYING THE CABLE FROM THE STERN OF THE "AGAMEMNON"

By this time the entire world was excited about the project, and most people believed that it was as good as done. The *Agamemnon* and *Niagara* set sail for Valentia on August 6, 1857. The huge cable was stored aboard, and cheering crowds watched their start. Bands played, flags were flying, and it seemed as if nothing could go wrong.

The end of the cable was laid at Valentia, and

immediately electricians in the *Niagara* began sending signals through it to the shore. As the cable
slowly slipped down into the sea from the laying-
out machine on deck, the messages continued
through its length.

Five miles out the cable broke, when the machinery for laying it jammed. A smaller boat was
able to bring up the broken end, which was spliced
to the cable on ship, and the procession started
again.

All went well for three days. This was a job that
had never been done before, and the men working
the machinery had to learn as they worked. The
laying-out machine and the speed of the ship had
to be watched constantly. Any sudden strain or jar
on the cable might snap it in two. Strong as it was,
it looked almost like a tiny thread as it slowly took
its way through the mighty ocean.

On the fourth day a storm arose. The *Niagara*
was carried off course by the wind, and the cable
was hard to manage as the ship rose and fell. The
cable had to be released slowly when the stern of
the ship sank in a wave, and payed out rapidly as

the stern rose. On the afternoon of that day, the ship rose too fast for the men in charge of the cable. It snapped, and the loose end sank down to the bottom of the sea.

There was no way to get it up. There was nothing to do but give up and return to shore. There was not enough cable left to start again from the beginning, and no more could be made before winter weather set in.

Most people believed that this failure proved that the plan would never work. It had seemed impossible in the first place—perhaps they had been carried away by enthusiasm for a while, but now their common sense was working again.

Mr. Bright was not discouraged. What had happened was not failure, but a chance to find out what had gone wrong. After all, the cable had been laid for three hundred miles without serious trouble, which proved that the basic idea was all right. He knew why it had broken, and would see that it did not happen again.

By the next summer he was ready for a new start. This time he had a different plan. Both ships

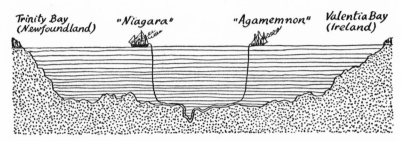

THE "NIAGARA" AND THE "AGAMEMNON" LAYING THE CABLE

would sail to mid-ocean, and the ends of the cable would be spliced. Each ship would then sail off, one for one shore and one for the other. This would let them lay the cable in much less time.

Before beginning the big project, the two ships went on a short practice trip. They spliced the cable, sailed away from each other, and then tried it again. They did this for several days until they believed they were ready to meet any problems of the big journey before them.

When they left port this time there were no bands, no cheering crowds, and no excitement. Almost everybody had lost interest because they expected another failure.

It soon appeared that those who doubted were

right. A terrible storm arose, and the *Agamemnon* was blown far off her course. Even worse than that, she was not built to carry a load as heavy as the cable, and for days it seemed as if she would be carried to the bottom of the ocean. Her seams opened, and she pitched from side to side in the terrible gales.

After many days the storm blew itself out, and the brave crew of the *Agamemnon* started back to the meeting spot in mid-ocean. They arrived there fifteen days later than had been planned. The weather was calm and sunny, and the ocean was as smooth as a mill pond.

The next morning the two ends of the cable were spliced and the ships sailed slowly away from each other. They had gone three miles when the cable broke.

Back they sailed, and tried again. This time sixty miles of cable had been laid out when it snapped.

On the next attempt, two hundred miles of cable were laid before it broke.

The situation was very bad. Both ships were

getting low on fuel and food. There was still enough cable left to complete the job, but what could they do if they ran out of coal when the job was almost completed? While the cable was being laid, each ship had to stay on course and keep moving at an even rate of speed. If a ship stopped, the cable would break.

They decided to try once more. This time, they agreed, they would stop if the cable broke after they had laid more than a hundred miles. Both ships would then go to the nearest port, Queenstown, Ireland.

The cable was spliced, and payed out smoothly from both ships. Perhaps now their bad luck was ended, and they would be able to finish the job. Hope rose again—and then the cable broke when the ships were one hundred and fourteen miles apart.

The *Agamemnon*, feeling that this was only a little more than the agreed length, went doggedly back to the mid-ocean meeting place. The *Niagara*, living up to the exact agreement, went to Queenstown. After several days, the *Agamemnon* realized what had happened, and sailed to join them there.

This is the most unbelievable part of the story. No one believed that an Atlantic cable could be laid—except the men who had suffered so much in trying to lay it.

Their minds were made up. They had started a job, and they intended to finish it. Once more both ships got ready to sail, while the whole world laughed at them.

When they left the harbor at Queenstown, on July 17, 1858, it seemed almost as if they were sneaking away, hoping not to be seen. They attracted no more attention than any ordinary ship, and no one cheered as they departed.

At mid-ocean, the cables were spliced, and the ships sailed away from each other. Day after day, during good weather and bad, they ploughed through the seas. The cable sank slowly down through the deep water, a thin line linking the ships.

Electricians on each ship signaled to each other through the cable. Most of the time the signals were regular and strong, but once in a while they stopped completely. No one dared stop to see what had gone wrong. If the cable was all right, stopping the ships would break it. On the chance that it was not a broken cable that stopped the signals, the ships kept on. Finally it was discovered that something was wrong with one of the sending mechanisms. This was repaired and the signals came through clearly again.

By this time, the men on board both ships began to believe that they were going to succeed. After all that had happened, how could they stand it if something went wrong now?

A shot from the cannon was to be the signal of disaster. Men working in the lower parts of the *Agamemnon* waited anxiously, hoping they would not hear the dread sound. Suddenly it rang out, and all work stopped. Men rushed on deck, crowding against the rail. The cable itself was still running smoothly into the sea—but ahead was something they could hardly believe. A passing ship was directly in front of them, and coming fast. Shots from the cannon rang out frantically in warning, and at the last minute the strange ship turned away.

Eight days after they had left the mid-ocean meeting place, both ships sailed into port. The trail they had left behind them, the Atlantic Cable, now linked two great continents.

The whole world caught fire with enthusiasm. People were as quick to cheer as they had been to criticize. Towns and cities celebrated, bonfires were lighted across both England and America. The men who had laid the cable were the greatest heroes in history. Messages flashed back and forth beneath the ocean. Success had come after one of the most difficult engineering jobs man had ever attempted.

This was in August. In October something began to go wrong. Signals through the cable became weaker and weaker and finally stopped altogether.

Once more the Atlantic Cable was a failure.

Mr. Cyrus Field, like Mr. Bright, refused to recognize failure. He began again to try to raise

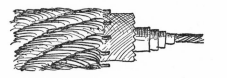

A SECTION OF THE MAIN CABLE 1865-66

money for a cable. Back and forth across the ocean he went, talking to men of wealth and asking their support. It was not an easy job, and it was made harder because Mr. Field suffered badly from sea-sickness. In spite of this, he crossed the ocean sixty-four times. Eventually he raised the money.

It had been easy to discover what had gone wrong. In their eagerness to send an electrical impulse strong enough to cover the distance, the electricians had used too much voltage. Perhaps if Mr. Bright had been able to get the stronger cable he wished, it would not have happened— but there was no use regretting past mistakes. The thing to do was to get a better cable, and to lay it over again.

By an odd chance, a ship that was exactly right for laying cable was ready to be used. The son of the engineer who dug the tunnel under the Thames had built a new kind of ship. Isambard Kingdom Brunel, also an engineer, had made it larger than almost any of its time, and with many un-usual features. It had the drawback of not being very practical for shipping most cargoes because it cost so much to run. Like the first Atlantic Cable, it was considered a failure.

This ship, the *Great Eastern,* was just what was needed for the unusual job of laying an Atlantic cable. It was so large and strong that it could do the job alone.

In July, 1866, the *Great Eastern* made a quiet, peaceful trip from one country to the other, and laid the entire cable.

Tying two continents together with a wire had taken time, money, and courage. Even more than this, it had taken engineers who would not admit that they had failed, but kept on until they had succeeded.

"THE GREAT EASTERN"

11

A BRIDGE THROWN ACROSS A RIVER

John Roebling said that he was going to throw a twenty-thousand-ton bridge across the East River in New York.

In 1850 the people of New York began to realize that a bridge should be built to connect Brooklyn and New York. Even in good weather it was a slow trip on the ferries, and when ice covered the river in winter the boats could not run at all.

The proposed bridge would have to be large, heavy and durable to take care of the traffic. Such bridges need strong heavy foundations.

Most bridge foundations are set in the bed of a river, and the bridge built on top of them. This could not be done in the East River because of the heavy boat traffic. The United States War Department said that any bridge would have to be at least one hundred thirty-five feet above the surface of the water, even while it was being built.

One kind of bridge has its foundations over it instead of beneath. This is called a suspension bridge.

A simple suspension bridge may be made by putting two cables across a river and then laying a light flooring between the cables. Another kind has tall towers or supports built on each side of a river, with cables connecting them. The bridge itself is hung from these cables.

It did not seem possible to put a suspension bridge across the East River because of the distance to be spanned. The longest suspension bridge in the world was only a little more than half as long as this one would have to be. Man had gone a long way since the days when the Greeks had been able to span a clear distance of only thirty feet, but who would believe that a span of sixteen hundred feet could be made?

John Roebling, a great bridge engineer, believed

that it could be done. He had started the first mill for making steel wire in this country, and had great faith in its strength. Until he began making steel cables for suspension bridges, heavy metal chains were used.

In 1857 he wrote a letter to the newspapers to suggest that a suspension bridge could be built across the East River. People were interested, but no one did anything about it for ten years. Then Mr. Roebling was offered the job.

Mr. Roebling knew what engineers mean when they say, "The big bridges are built under water." If the foundation of a bridge is not built properly, the bridge will not be any good. His big bridge would have to have an especially good foundation. In a bridge to be supported from beneath, the river bed must be dug out until solid rock is found. Even suspension bridges, which swing from tall supports, must be held by strong foundations which are set on solid rock. Usually, building any large bridge means that supports must be set beneath the water, whether in the river bed or on the bank.

Men cannot stand under water and dig. Even

if they could, the current of the water would fill up the hole as fast as it was dug out.

To solve this problem engineers invented a box which could be lowered into water and then pumped dry. Men could work inside this box, lowering it as they dug deeper. This box is called a caisson.

Think of a very strong box with four sides and a top, but no bottom. It is towed by boat to above the place where it is to rest, and then weighted until the lower edges sit on the river bottom.

Water trapped inside is pumped out by forcing compressed air into the caisson. Water is normally much heavier than air, but air can be squeezed or compressed until it is heavier than water. As long as the caisson is kept filled with compressed air, water cannot get back inside.

Mr. Roebling intended to use caissons for digging the foundations of his bridge, but he knew that they were dangerous. Men's bodies were not made to live in compressed air, and it causes difficulties. The rapid change from normal to compressed air

MEN WORKING INSIDE A CAISSON

causes a condition called the bends, which can be fatal.

To avoid this, air locks were made through which the men had to pass on their way in and out of the caissons. In each air lock the air was slightly less compressed than in the caisson so the men's bodies were gradually accustomed to the change in air pressure. Every workman was ordered to use the air locks, but people do not always do what they are told. There were many cases of the bends, or caisson disease.

John Roebling himself was the victim of an accident. While he was working at the site of the bridge his foot was crushed, infection set in, and he died before the bridge was even started.

His son, Washington Roebling, immediately took over the job. Two huge caissons, one on each side of the river, were set in place. One of them had to be lowered to a depth of eighty feet below high water level before a solid foundation of rock was found.

The other caisson ran into trouble almost at once. Fire broke out in it, and Washington Roebling worked so desperately that he forgot precautions. He became ill with the dreaded caisson disease.

In spite of this, the work was carried on. When Mr. Roebling was not well enough to leave his room he watched progress from the window of his home, and sent instructions by messenger.

As soon as a good foundation had been reached, work was begun on two giant towers. They were one hundred and forty feet by sixty feet at the water line, and rose one hundred and eighteen feet above that into the air.

At this point, each tower was divided into three smaller pillars forming two arches which rose two hundred and thirty-eight feet and six inches above the water. This was before the skyscrapers of New York had been built, and the towers of the bridge rose high above anything else in sight.

When these immense pillars were completed, the foundation of the bridge was laid. It was time to string the huge cables which would support the bridge. These are called spun cables, which sounds as if they were twisted together like the strands of a rope. Mr. Roebling knew that a cable made of wires lying close together, but not twisted, is stronger, so his spun cables were not what their name suggests. He invented a new way of making these cables, which must carry a terrific weight.

Two slender wire ropes were strung between the towers, and a light foot walk was suspended from them. A trolley, or sheave, which held a loop of cable wire, was run back and forth along the two wire ropes. On each trip, this loop meant that two strands of cable were put in place, and two hundred and seventy-eight trips were made before the cable was completed.

The finished cable was made of 5,296 galvanized

steel oil-coated wires, laid side by side and wrapped in the form of a cylinder. It was fifteen and three-fourths inches across and weighed almost one thousand tons. This was a time when the material had to be finished on the job, rather than prepared somewhere else. If the cable had been made before it was to be put up, there would have been no way to lift it to the tops of the towers.

A TEST TRIP ON THE FIRST CABLE BETWEEN THE TOWERS

More heavy wire ropes, called suspenders, were hung from the large cables to hold the floor beams of the bridge. Some of them went straight down, and others were added which slanted from the tops of the towers to the floor of the bridge. The extra ones from the towers were strong enough to hold the bridge even if the others broke. Mr. Roebling was taking no chances.

It was fourteen years before the bridge was finished, and it was so beautiful that people could hardly believe it. Mr. Roebling had not intended to make one of the most beautiful bridges in the world, but one of the best. It often happens that something designed well for a certain purpose turns out to be beautiful.

It was the longest suspension bridge in the world when it was finished, and proved that John Roebling had been right. The Brooklyn Bridge still stands today, and is used by millions of people.

Mr. Roebling and his father gave the city of New York a wonderful bridge, but he gave the world something more than that. When you ride across one of the great bridges in our country, remember the engineer who gave us the steel cable, and proved that the mind of man is greater than any river.

ONE OF THE MOST BEAUTIFUL BRIDGES IN THE WORLD